A TOILET PAPER

A TOILET PAPER

OR

A TREATISE ON FOUR FUNDAMENTAL WORDS
REFERRING TO GASEOUS AND SOLID WASTES
TOGETHER WITH THEIR POINT OF ORIGIN

RACHEL MINES

Published by
Anvil Press
#204-A 175 East Broadway,
Vancouver, B.C.
CANADA V5T 1W2

2nd Revised Edition: November, 2001.

CANADIAN CATALOGUING IN PUBLICATION DATA
Mines, Rachel.
A toilet paper
(Anvil small book series, ISSN 1188-1623 ; no. 1)
Includes bibliographical references.
ISBN 1-895636-40-X

1. English language—Obscene words. 2. English language—Etymology. 3. Scatology—
Humor. I. Title. II. Title: A treatise on four fundamental words referring to gaseous and
solid wastes. III. Series.
PE1583.M55 1991   422   C92-091003-3

ANVIL SMALL BOOK SERIES NO. 1 (ISSN: 1188-1623)
Cover design: Rayola Graphic Design
Cover & interior illustrations: Geneviève Castrée
Printed and bound in Canada.

Represented in Canada by the Literary Press Group/Distributed by General Distribution

The publisher gratefully acknowledges the financial assistance of the B.C. Arts Council,
the Canada Council for the Arts, and the Book Publishing Industry Development
Program (BPIDP) for their support of our publishing program.

To my daughter, Sarah who at the tender age of six demonstrated her mastery of the Magic Word:

  –Pass the ketchup.
  –What do you say? What's the Magic Word?
  –Pass the fucking ketchup.

And to Gernot Wieland, who encouraged my love of Old English. Wæs þu hal!

TABLE OF CONTENTS

INTRODUCTION

*T*HE INVISIBLE IS as present as the visible. The space between things—stars, chess pieces, words on a page—defines existence as much as does the thing itself. Without the featureless background of this paper, you would not be reading these words. Where there is no ground, no figure is possible. An object is characterized by what it is not, as much as by what it is. So, too, it is with language.

Gaps, blank spaces in the language of polite conversation—academic discourse being but one example—are linguistic manifestations of human psychology. They are like black holes into which we conveniently drop undesirable concepts referring to things we fear on the deepest levels, things we would rather not face without a hedge of psychological defences: sex, death, bodily wastes, things unmentionable in polite society. But these things do not go away by virtue of their unmentionability; and neither do the words referring to them, though most are now relegated to the status of street language, slang, or 'obscenity'.

This small book is an attempt to examine, from a historical linguistic viewpoint, four words relating to our posterior orifice and that which comes out of it. None of these words is a recent coinage; all, in fact, are part of our deeply-rooted linguistic heritage, traceable back to the Indo-European language spoken about 5,000 years ago, of which modern English is a direct descendant.

WARNING!!!

The following pages are entirely concerned with words referring to bodily elimination. This material is not suitable for young children. If you are easily shocked or offended by frank discussion or orthographical representation (including charts and I.P.A. transcriptions) of words referring to certain bodily processes, DO NOT TURN THIS PAGE!

And up the wyndow dide he hastely
And out his erse he putteth pryvely.

—CHAUCER, MILLER'S TALE

Marry, sir, you must send the ass upon the horse,
for he is very slow-gaited.

—SHAKESPEARE, LOVE'S LABOUR'S LOST

There was a young woman named Glass
Who had a most beautiful ass
Not round and pink
As you might think
But grey, and had ears, and ate grass.

—MONTAGU

$\mathcal{A}$LTHOUGH THIS IS probably the mildest and least offensive of the so-called dirty words, neither my pocket-size Bantam Dictionary nor my Roget's Thesaurus has any mention of its American cousin ass (in the gluteal, not the quadrupedal sense). Needless to say, neither of these fine tomes contain any dirty words at all, as far as I can see (and I've looked); which is some indication of the difficulty inherent in dirty word research; many indexers seem to consistently ignore them, perhaps in the hope that they'll eventually go away.

15

However, this fundamental word has a pedigree quite as long and distinguished as those of more refined vocables.

ETYMOLOGY AND SOUND CHANGE: ARSE

I. THE FAMILY TREE

Indo-European root		*ars-	(variant)*ors-
	Germanic	*arsoz	Greek orrhos
Old English		ears, ærs	
Middle English		ars, ers	
Modern English		arse, ass	

SOUND CHANGES FROM OLD ENGLISH

From the Old English masculine noun *ears* /ɛars/, variant *ærs* /ærs/, both /ɛa/ and /æ/ shift to /a/, giving us Middle English *ars*. Chaucer's usage *ers* was a variation typical of the London dialect; and by about 1500, both variants would be pronounced /ars/. At about this time, or even in the late Middle English period, according to Ekwall[1], /r/ was sometimes lost, especially before /s/; the /a/ later fronts to /æ/ during the Great Vowel Shift of the 15th Century; and sure enough, upon checking several concordances to Shakespeare, I found references only to *ass*. Our North American usage must descend from this, much to the delight of several generations of schoolchildren: *Why do they call Jesus the Incredible Rubber Man? He tied his ass to a tree and walked to Jerusalem!* Our less privileged British friends, alas, are no longer privy to such a glorious state of affairs. After the end of the eighteenth century, Pyles[2] tells us, the British /æ/ shifts to /a/ in a number of frequently used words. *Ass* must have been one such; the spelling reverted to *arse* and the pronunciation is now /a:s/.

Usage

As well as the unadorned nouns *arse* or *ass*, history offers us a good many interesting compounds, ranging from the pithy to the (almost) poetic. Bosworth's *Anglo-Saxon Dictionary* includes, among others: *earse-ende* (conjuring images of poor little Godric's after being caught sticky-fingered in the honey jar); the adverb *on earsling*, meaning 'backward' (even today, many of us, in our more addled moments, may find ourselves doing things *ass-backward*, or even *back-assward*); or, my favourite, *ears-þerl*: 'þerl = þyrel, a hole'. Nice to know the Anglo-Saxons had them, too.

The *Middle English Dictionary*, along with some rather pithy quotes, gives us: *arsgang* (a bowel movement); *arshol* (did they hurl this term of abuse at annoying neighbours, do you think?); and *arswisp*: 'the medieval equivalent of toilet paper'. By Shakespeare's time, as noted above, the words *arse* and *ass* have fallen together, setting the stage for many an asinine pun; and in American usage the two words are often confounded to this day. (*N.B.*: *Our four-legged friend derives from the Indo-European root *ans-, evolving to Old English assa, Middle English asse.*)

According to Montagu[3], *arse* was Standard English for buttocks until about 1660, thereafter becoming a vulgarism. The *Oxford English Dictionary* lists it as 'obsolete in polite use', but *arse* and its North American variant *ass* are still alive and kicking in contemporary idiomatic speech.

FART

This Nicholas anoon leet fle a fart
As greet as it hadde been a thonder dent.

—CHAUCER, MILLER'S TALE

Fart. Not in decent use.

—OXFORD ENGLISH DICTIONARY

*L*IKE A BAD SMELL, this word just doesn't go away. Beloved by Chaucer, unused by Shakespeare, 'fart' has long endured, heard but not seen, to give pleasure to yet another generation of English-speakers, most of whom know the value of a pungent word better than do their own publishers.

ETYMOLOGY AND SOUND CHANGES: FART

I. THE FAMILY TREE

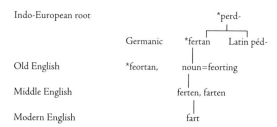

Indo-European root   *perd-

Germanic   *fertan   Latin péd-

Old English   *feortan,   noun=feorting

Middle English   ferten, farten

Modern English   fart

22   SOUND CHANGES FROM OLD ENGLISH

The Old English verb *feortan is reconstructed from the feminine noun feorting; although Partridge's Origins[4] does not indicate it as a reconstruction (Skeat[5] doesn't even list it), the verb does not itself appear in the Old English dictionaries. I could find neither noun nor verb in Somner's[6] 1659 dictionary; but Lye's[7] 1772 dictionary lists feorting, as does the Anglo-Saxon Dictionary and Clark-Hall's Concise Anglo-Saxon Dictionary.

At any rate, both Partridge and the Oxford English Dictionary agree that the Indo-European root was *perd-. Grimm's Law shifts the /p/ to /f/ and the /d/ to /t/, giving us the Germanic *fertan*/fɛrtan/; full breaking shifts the /ɛ/ to /ɛɔ/, giving us the Old English *feortan*/fɛɔrtan/. I was unable to determine whether this was a strong or weak verb; at any rate, it is weak in modern usage.

By the Middle English period, /ɛɔ/ has reverted to /ɛ/, yielding *ferten*/fɛrtən/; by Early Modern English the /ɛ/ has shifted to /a/ before /r/. Interestingly, Chaucer has *fart* well before this time, as, conversely, he has *ers* where we would expect *ars*. It seems that the /r/ must affect the preceding vowel, and perhaps /a/ and /ɛ/ in this position were somewhat interchangeable. By the Early Modern English period, anyway, whether spelled with *a* or *e*, the pronunciation would have been *fart*, the vowel later lengthening (again, due to the vocalic quality of the /r/) to /faːrt/.

USAGE

The Old English dictionaries politely define *feorting* as 'crepitus ventris'. We receive little further enlightenment until the Middle English period, when *fart* comes into its own, at least in a literary sense. The *Middle English Dictionary* gives us such colourful terms as *leten flien a fart*, to break wind; *not worth a fart*; and the noun *farter*, a worthless person. Chaucer's use of the word is either positively scandalous or absolutely hilarious, depending on one's viewpoint.

Much to my dismay, though Shakespeare puns on *wind instruments* and *tails* in *Othello* (Act III, Scene I), he apparently does not use the word *fart* at all; at least I couldn't find it in any of the several concordances I checked. This is an unfortunate illustration of the difficulty of dirty-word research; it is sometimes impossible to know if a word truly does not exist in a work, or if it has been omitted from word-lists due to editorial squeamishness.

Montagu's *Anatomy of Swearing* tells us that *fart* was Standard English to the mid-eighteenth century (if so, its non-use by Shakespeare is yet more surprising). Modern idiomatic usage is mostly confined to that of schoolchildren (*Fartface!*). In hopes of returning *fart* to its former glory, therefore, I would like to propose a revival of the term *fartsucker*, 'in use in the late nineteenth and early twentieth century for a parasite.'[8]

I was surprised to discover that *fart* has a little-known cognate in English: one that is idiomatic, used in only one fixed sense, and usually misunderstood. I refer to the word *petard*, used by Shakespeare in *Hamlet* (Act III, Scene III): 'For 'tis the sport to have the engineer/hoist with his own petard . . .' The petard is not an esoteric species of rope or ship's rigging (until recently, I thought it was employed to string up unruly sailors), but was an explosive device 'fired with gunpowder, which was used to demolish obstacles. It was frequently hoisted up to destroy obstacles at a high level; but it was such an infernal machine that anyone who had the unfortunate task of firing it stood in great danger of losing their own life.'—Ewart[9].

Petard, like *fart*, comes to us from the Indo-European root **perd-*; from this we get the Latin *pēdere*, to break wind, which gives us *pēditium* and the Medieval French *pet*, which yields the verb *peter*, to explode. Thus Early Modern French *pétard* literally means 'explosive' or 'farter'.

'Scitan: to go to ſtoole to ſy—'
—DICTIONARIUM SAXICO-LATINO-
ANGLICUM, 1659

And shame it is, if a preest take keepe
A shiten sheperde and a clene sheep.
—CHAUCER, PROLOGUE TO THE
CANTERBURY TALES

Those who write on bathroom walls
Roll their shit in little balls.
Those who read such lines of wit
Eat those little balls of shit.
—LATE 20TH CENTURY bathroom grafitti

THIS ANCIENT, WELL-LOVED WORD, though lamentably absent from most classroom dictionaries, not only has a blue-blood pedigree, but claims a number of close relations that are freely admitted into the most respectable of circles. In fact, most people who substitute '*Shoot!*' in polite conversation are blissfully unaware that, as George Carlin puts it, 'Shoot is simply shit with two o's' (quoted in Christopher).[10] What's wrong with *shit*? There is scanty but thought-provoking evidence that the word might be an essential part of our very human nature; not only do many flight recorders recovered from downed aircraft reveal a despondent '*Shit!*' from the pilot moments before impact, but Washoe, a chimp trained in American Sign Language, spontaneously transformed the matter-of-fact noun into a pejorative when annoyed with her trainer. Volumes have been written on the subject of shit, from the agricultural to the psychological to the technological. Shit is as essential to life as breathing itself; though we can go without food for a month, sleep for a week, and water for three or four days, anyone who doesn't shit every twenty-four hours or so is courting a stomach ache. It is strange that we should have, as a society, such a deeply embedded fear of 'poo-poo-kaka' (as my friend Daphne the Environmentalist puts it), that we dare not speak its name.

Etymology and Sound Changes: Shit

I. THE FAMILY TREE

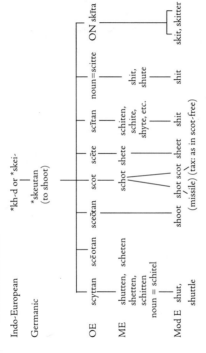

Partridge cites evidence for the Indo-European root *kh-d, 'to cast or throw'; Old Slavic *is-kydati* means 'to cast out'. The Germanic /sk/, he states, reinforces the Indo-European /k/; while Grimm's Law would modulate the /d/ to /t/. Skeat traces only as far back as *skeutan*; and the *Oxford English Dictionary* states that 'the affinities outside Teutonic are doubtful.' Fleming, in her *Analysis of a Four-Letter Word*[11], cites *The American Heritage Dictionary* in giving the Indo-European root *skei-*, meaning 'to cut or split'.

All agree, however, on the Germanic *skeutan*, meaning 'to shoot'. Direct descendants into Old English are *scyttan*, to shoot a bolt, that is, to shut; *sceōtan*, and its variant (from which our modern form *shoot* is derived) *sceōtan*, to shoot; the nouns *scot*, a shot; and *scēte*, a sheet; the Old Norse *skīta*, from which we derive *skit* and *skitter*; and, of course, *scītan* and its corresponding *scitte*.

Sound Changes from Old English

The Old English Class I verb *scītan*/šitan/ has a corresponding feminine noun, *scitte*/šɪtːe/: diarrhea, or, as Somner's quaintly puts it, 'a fluxe or looseness of the belly'.[12] From this we get Middle English *shit*/šɪt/, which is, of course, identical to our Modern English word.

The verb *scītan* retains virtually the same pronunciation in Middle English, /šitən/, although the spelling changes somewhat: *schiten*, *shiten*, or the variants with the 'y' rather than the 'i' spelling. Had the verb followed the usual Class I pattern of sound changes, the 'i' would shift to /əi/ and later /aɪ/ starting in the Early Modern period; and indeed the *Oxford English Dictionary* gives us the modern variant *shite*/šaɪt/, which is largely obsolete. The Modern English verb *shit* is thus probably derived from the noun or the regular development of the Old English past participle, *sciten*/šɪtɛn/.

The past tense of the verb presents several problems. Regular development of the Old English past tense *scāt*/šat/ gives us Middle English *shot(e)*/šɔːt/; which appears thus in the *Middle English Dictionary*. However, further development into

33

Modern English would yield the diphthongized *shote*/šoʊt/; this may well be the past tense of the older variant *shite*, but it is certainly not in use today.

In fact, there seems to be no less than three contenders for the preterite of *shit*. The regular weak form, *shitted*, seems to be little used by those beyond childhood; at least in an informal Sunday afternoon neighbourhood poll, this form garnered nary a vote; people seem about equally divided between 'shit' (8 votes) and 'shat' (9 votes). Interestingly, about half of those polled informed me that their preferred term is 'took a shit', which enables them to get around the problem entirely; they cast a vote for one of the alternatives only after being (gently) pressed.

Fitzjames,[13] in his 1978 *Maledicta* article, reports that the results of his literature survey show a preponderance of *shit* forms from the Middle Ages to the mid-twentieth century. Thus the *shat* form may be a modern construction analagous to the preterites of *sit* and *spit*. It is an interesting coincidence that this form is almost identical to the Old English past tense, which is thus back in service after a hiatus of almost a millenium.

Usage

Montagu tells us that *shit* was used as Standard English for excrement 'from the sixteenth to the early nineteenth century.'[14] Obviously he does not go back far enough; nonetheless, I found no colourful compounds or instances of idiomatic usage in either Old or Middle English. Even the single quote of Chaucer's I was able to unearth refers merely to 'a shiten shepherde and a clene sheepe,' which is metaphorical, but does not attain the height (or depth) of the colourful idiom employed today. I could not find a single example in Shakespeare, though Fleming cites several quotes from the sixteenth and seventeenth centuries. It is probably at about this time that the word began to be deemed obscene, for it is sometimes spelled with dashes in place of letters. Montagu states that the compounds *shitarse*, *shitbag*, *shitpot*, are all nineteenth century in origin.

Modern idiomatic usages of the word are far too numerous to mention more than a handful here. Christopher, in his *A Taboo-Boo Word Revisited*, lists seven categories of usage, including the literal: *take a shit* (but once you've taken it, *then* what do you do with it?); the figurative: *the shit hit the fan*, and animal metaphors such as *bullshit* and *chickenshit*; insults: *shithead, stupid shit*, etc.; fear: *scare the shit out of*; and grammatical intensifiers and interjections: *holy shit, oh shit*, and the ever-reliable *shit!*

36

Đaer þū gesēo tordwifel on eorþan up weorpan, ymbfo hine mid twā handum mid his geweorpe.

—ANGLO-SAXON DICTIONARY

They shul be shryned in an hogges toord.

—CHAUCER, PARDONER'S TALE

If there be one or two, I shall make-a de turd.

—SHAKESPEARE, MERRY WIVES OF WINDSOR

*L*IKE *shit*, *turd* has a large number of cognates, or words descended from the same root. Unlike the other words we have so far examined, however, there is a romantic air about *turd* (if we may use that particular expression), since it is derived from Latin, and thus enjoys a variety of French cousins, some of whom later emigrated back into English. A truly cosmopolitan word, widely travelled in the best linguistic circles, *turd*, like a dowdy but genteel old woman living in quiet retirement after a lifetime of globe-trotting, deserves far more respect and recognition than it is given today.

39

The Indo-European root of turd is uncertain; though the Oxford English Dictionary gives **drto-*, Partridge's *Origins* cites **trokw-*, which by metathesis gives the Latin stem *torq-*, meaning 'to twist.' As well as *turd*, from Latin *torquēre* descend our Modern English *contort(ion)*, *distort(ion)*, *extort(ion)*, and *retort*.

To think that a lowly 'twist of shit' has such exalted relations!

40

1. THE FAMILY TREE

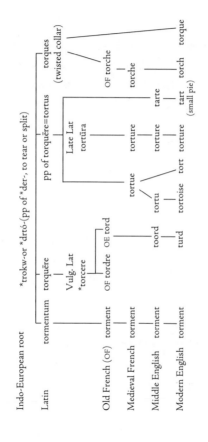

Indo-European root		*trokw-or *drtó-(pp of *der-, to tear or split)		
Latin	tormentum	torquēre	pp of torquēre=tortus	torques (twisted collar)
		Vulg. Lat *torcere	Late Lat tortūra	OF torche
Old French (OF)	torment	OF tordre	OE tord	tortue — torche — tarte — torture
Medieval French	torment		roord	tortu — torture — tarte
Middle English	torment			tortoise — tort — torture — tart (small pie)
Modern English	torment		turd	torch — torque

SOUND CHANGES FROM OLD ENGLISH

From the Old English neuter noun *tord*/tɔrd/ we get Middle English *toord*/tord/, the consonant cluster lengthening the /ɔ/ in the first phase of lengthening. Chaucer obligingly gives us the spelling *toord*. After 1350, the vowel again becomes short /ɔ/. I am unable to determine, however, how this /ɔ/ shifts to /u/, but shift it has by the Early Modern period, since Shakespeare's spelling is *turd*; by then the /ʊ/ had shifted again due to the r+ consonant cluster, yielding /tɜrd/, which is still our Modern English pronunciation.

42

USAGE

Turd, in usage, has never achieved the scatological splendour of *shit*, but has largely remained an everyday term for a piece of dung, usually of animal origin. The *Anglo-Saxon Dictionary* lists, among others: *swines* and *horses tord*, *gates* (goat) *tord*, and *tord-wifel*, or dung beetle. The *Middle English Dictionary*, much to my chagrin, has not yet published volume T; however, we find some slightly more colourful usage in Chaucer, such as: 'Thy drasty rymyng is nat worth a toord,' in the *Tale of Melibeus*.

Shakespeare puns once on the word; in the *Merry Wives of Windsor* (Act III Scene III) Caius says, '*If there be one or two, I shall make-a de turd*'—punning on third.

Current usage is mostly confined to the prosaic rather than the metaphorical, a recent (and unfortunately recurring) example from my own household being: 'Look at all these mouse turds on the counter!' We may remark on the occasional dog turd on the sidewalk, but the word is rarely used as a term of abuse; indeed, in other than literal usage, it is scarcely interchangeable with *shit*; we may call someone a 'turd', but 'scared turdless' or 'oh, turd!' somehow just don't make it.

This constriction of meaning may be due to two factors: first, *turd* is a noun only, where *shit* is also a verb; second, *shit* is a collective noun, whereas '*turd refers to the individuation of shit*.'[15]
—Phúc-Dông.

43

I cannot pretend to understand why the ordinary Anglo-Saxon words for bodily elimination have within the last few centuries become taboo. Perhaps it was due to a potent combination of religious repression and delusions of cultural grandeur; at any rate, that's a topic for a paper—or a book—of its own. What I do know is that while many of these words are uttered freely in colloquial or idiomatic speech, there are vast areas of everyday life in which they are unacknowledged, virtually non-existent. Although some of the more recent dictionaries are once again starting to include them, most academic discourse—published articles, classroom conversation, and the average university research paper—is generally 'clean'. But dirty words have always been with us; and I believe it is time to reclaim this important part of our linguistic tradition.

Why study dirty words? Well, to paraphrase Terence, *'I am a member of the human race; nothing human is alien to me.'* That's one good reason. But another, less lofty though just as human, is the perverse sense of glee I must admit in using the tools of academia—dictionaries, concordances, literary works—in

44

pursuit of what to many is a base ideal. One of my fondest childhood memories is the smell of a new paperback dictionary, inky and virtually warm from the press in my hand; myself at the wooden, ink-scarred classroom desk, flipping through those fragrant pages, in search of the elusive, never-found *dirty word* (the joy be in the quest, not the attainment). Imagine, then, my delight on a recent rainy afternoon at the information desk in the Ridington Room of the U.B.C. Main Library, when upon being asked by the librarian for precisely *which* word I was searching for in the *Middle English Dictionary* (unbound issues being at the desk), with what unalloyed joy I stood a little straighter, held my head a little higher, and (stammering only slightly), proudly answered: *SHIT!*

45

Works Cited

1. Ekwall, Eilert. *A History of Modern English Sounds and Morphology.*
   Translated by Alan Ward. Totawa, New Jersey: Rowman, 1975.

2. Pyles, Thomas, and Alego, John. *The Origins and Development of the
   English Language.* 3rd ed. San Diego: Harcourt, 1982.

3. Montagu, Ashley. *The Anatomy of Swearing.* New York: Macmillan,
   1967.

4. Partridge, Eric. *Origins: A Short Etymological Dictionary of Modern English.*
   New York: Greenwich, 1983.

5. Skeat, Walter. *Etymological Dictionary of the English Language.* Oxford:
   Clarendon Press, 1958.

6. Somner, William. *Dictionarium Saxonico-Latino-Anglicum.* Reprint ed.
   Menston: Scolar Press, 1970.

7. Lye, Eduardo. *Dictionarium Saxonico-Latino-Anglicum.* London: B. White,
   1772.

8. Montagu, Ashley. (op. cit.)

9. Ewart, Neil. *Everyday Phrases.* Poole: Blandford Press, 1983.

10. Christopher, Richard. 'A Taboo-Boo Word Revisited'. *Maledicta* 3
    (1979): 195-196.

11. Fleming, Margaret. 'Analysis of a Four-Letter Word'. *Maledicta* 1
    (1977): 173-184.

12. Somner, William. (op. cit.)

13. Fitzjames, DelHole. 'On the Indirect Resolution . . .' *Maledicta* 2
    (1978): 121-128.

14. Montagu, Ashley. (op. cit.)

15. Phúc-Dông, Quang. 'Three Lexicograhic Notes on Individuation'. *Maledicta* 1 (1977): 75-76.

Other Sources Cited

1. *An Anglo-Saxon Dictionary*. Oxford: Clarendon, 1898.

2. Chaucer, Geoffrey. *The Canterbury Tales*. Facsimile ed. Folkstone: Wm. Dawson and Sons, 1979.

3. Clark-Hall, J.R. *A Concise Anglo-Saxon Dictionary*, 4th ed. Toronto: University of Toronto Press, 1960.

4. *Compact Edition of the Oxford English Dictionary*. Oxford: Oxford University Press, 1971.

5. *Middle English Dictionary*. Ann Arbor: University of Michigan Press, 1954.

6. Shakespeare, William. *The Complete Works*. London: Hamlyn, 1958.

Rachel Mines has a PhD in English from King's College, University of London (UK). After realizing, much to her dismay, that the world is not crying out for specialists in Old English poetic meter, she surrendered to the inevitable and turned to the corporate sector. She now operates her own writing and editing business.

Rachel also teaches English at UBC, provides online instruction for an award-winning business writing course offered to UN employees, and is on the marking team for the LPI, an English placement exam dreaded by legions of BC undergrads. She is that rarest of entities: a resident of Vancouver who was actually born and raised there.